FEATHERED FRIENDS

Experience the day-to-day events of this diverse community of feathered friends and one friend not so feathered

CONSTANCE GLIDDEN JOSEF

ISBN 979-8-89130-567-0 (paperback)
ISBN 979-8-89130-568-7 (digital)

Christian Faith Publishing
832 Park Avenue
Meadville, PA 16335
www.christianfaithpublishing.com

Printed in the United States of America

To Conrad, my soulmate and dearest friend and husband, thank you. Conrad joined me every night to enjoy watching and listening to the glorious array of feathered friends. Conrad also contributed to the story with ideas for added photographs.

To all of the birds who joined us every night for evening treats and the frolicking that always took place before and after: families of Canada geese, mallard ducks, herons, egrets (tall and small), and the periodic appearance of an ibis. Eight wonderful years, every evening, regardless of the weather, these feathered friends would gather around the landing, the opening to the building where Bird Lady lived. Bird Lady came down every evening with her bag of evening treats (cracked corn, dried wild bird nuts and fruits, and goose and duck special blend). All of the birds would wait for Bird Lady's arrival and let her know with honks and quacks if she was late! As Bird Lady came out to join them, all the birds would gather around and follow her to each of the spots for evening treats.

You'll come to learn throughout the story that *we* humans are the lucky ones to have the many feathered friends among us. The feathered ones will always show their fondness for you when you give your kindness.

Bird Lady

E
NTERING THE QUIET community of feathered friends, one immediately sees the diversity of those who reside here, and it's especially interesting seeing the relaxed and peaceful looks that appear among their togetherness for the variety of ducks and geese under the shade of the trees. They don't distance themselves from each other, no matter what species of bird.

Both ponds (north and south) display the tranquility of these quiet feathered friends: ducks, geese, heron, egrets (tall and small), and ibis. There seems to be a companionship among the different feathered friends. They share the quietness of the tree-shaded, grassy pond slopes as family and friends.

They enjoy togetherness even in the ponds. There is no fighting but rather playful fun. They eat what they may find of the many acorns, grass, and aquatic plants—nourishment for all.

It didn't seem unusual to see the ducks swimming among the geese nor seeing the ducks and geese enjoying the evening grain treat (mix of cracked corn, nuts and fruit mix, and goose and duck feed) that was provided by Bird Lady.

Bird Lady comes out every evening, before sunset, and is greeted by the ducks and geese. Some would waddle right up to her to show their comfort and joy to see her.

They also enjoy showing off their new babies. Mother Duck in front, looking back at her proud parade of baby ducklings.

The tall, lanky heron always walks along the edge of the pond to join everyone gathered about the evening grain treats of cracked corn, mixed in with goose and duck grains.

Of course, you could also hear the goose periodically cry out from being goosed by their fellow goose friend—their way of picking on each other. A pull of a goose's feather on the backside would always cause a ruckus. A pluck of feathers will be dangling from the angry goose's mouth, while the plucked goose would look back and paddle even faster into the pond, screaming back. All of the geese would go scattering back out into the pond, as if to think they might be next. And of course, the ducks would take advantage of the openings in front of the treats of pleasure and enjoy eating more before the geese returned.

There's nothing better than a goose fight to give the ducks more treat bits. But then, calm would overtake the geese, realizing that if they wanted evening treats, they better head back and stop the fighting.

Once everyone had enjoyed their bit of evening treat, they would gather along the south pond's edge in front of Bird Lady, looking out upon them from her veranda. Sometimes, Bird Lady would sit among them or up on her veranda, looking across all of them. Whether they sat quietly or were napping, bathing or just swimming, and sometimes showing off, they were together.

They knew each other and found happiness in their surroundings. This sight was Bird Lady's evening treat. Happiness and flocking among all—what better way to end the day than for everyone to know they had friends among themselves.

When evening came upon us, each Canada goose family would start gathering in their V formation for departure.

The lead male goose would call out (honking sound), drawing upon the families' attention that it was time to leave for the night. The honking sound was repeated many times to ensure the family members and everyone around the pond knew they would be departing.

They didn't sleep at the pond but rather in the woods. The call-out would have the Canada goose lead at the tip of the V formation. The family members would paddle out into formation.

The Canada goose lead would lead them, flying out of the pond, making a clear goose honk for all to hear his announcement that they were leaving for the night. There were always at least three or four families. Sometimes the family members were as many as eight or as few as two.

This was an every-night ritual, regardless of the number of Canada goose family members. Every Canada goose family performed their callout to ready for departure, and the lead Canada goose would form the tip of the V and fly, leading them out of the pond and up over the trees, always continuing to announce the families' departure.

Goodnight to all.

For several weeks, there had been a lot of construction work occurring all around the community. What was once groves of trees and wild bushes were now being dozed under. The wild-at-heart residents of those areas were being forced out. It would be difficult to know just what would be coming to join the feathered friends.

On a Saturday afternoon, while walking home, after Bird Lady's morning jog, she came upon a new family of Canada geese walking down the sidewalk that ran alongside of the community where Bird Lady lived. The family did not fear Bird Lady's presence and simply demonstrated they were walking to find a place to stay, not so unusual with all of the woodland being destroyed.

Walking in a single file was the mother goose, followed by three young baby geese and the father goose. Bird Lady walked up to the mother goose and asked, "Where are you going?"

The mother goose looked across the brick wall, as if to say, "Looking for a way to get in." Well, there was no way to walk in there, but Bird Lady knew she could take them across the street to her community with the two large ponds and lots of feathered friends to meet.

Bird Lady then led the mother goose and the entire family across the street. Bird Lady stopped traffic and, with her arms outstretched, made sure the family stayed together as she herded them across the street and up to the community entry. Bird Lady walked them to the top of the pond's grassy knoll. The Canada goose family of five gathered around Bird Lady and looked down at the pond.

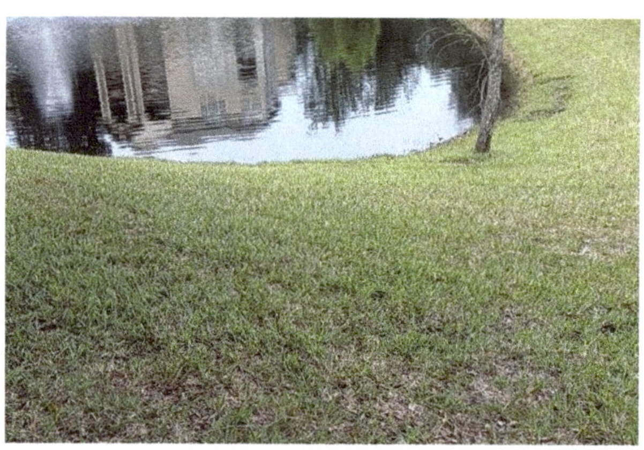

Suddenly, the father goose outstretched his wings and ran to the pond and jumped in.

One of the little geese followed and jumped in after its dad. The mother goose, along with her other two littles ones, stood beside Bird Lady. The mother goose looked up at Bird Lady, as if to say, "Thank you. I hope this can become our home." The mother goose and her two little ones then walked down to the edge of the pond and jumped in to enjoy. Bird Lady felt such happiness seeing the family join her feathered family and looked forward to coming to know them and watch how they would be welcomed into the community of feathered friends.

It was a fun time for the entire family. They joined the other ducks in the community for evening treats and enjoyed the grassy knolls during the day. Everyone welcomed them.

There was playful fun among the baby geese and ducks.

As the days went by, the baby geese were quickly growing. One day, Bird Lady noticed one of the babies was limping. One leg appeared shorter than the other. Researching appearance on Google brought the understanding that female Canada geese can inherit a DNA problem that causes a leg to be shorter. Over time, the shorter leg will catch up with the other, but it can pose difficulties for the babies as they are growing. And indeed, it did. One morning, Bird Lady noticed the family enjoying the morning sun under the shade of the corner trees and shrubs. Bird Lady also saw one of the babies face down in the water. Running, Bird Lady hoped to save the little one, but it was not meant to be. Bird Lady cradled the little one out of the water. So very sad was Bird Lady. It was such a little goose who had just been joining in on fun in the pond yesterday. The little one may have tripped and fell in the water and, unfortunately, drowned. Bird Lady laid the little one next to the mother goose so she could get a shovel. Bird Lady then laid to rest the baby girl goose behind the shrubs, where her Canada goose family always set, so the little one could be with her family in spirit. Although Bird Lady was so saddened by the event, she could look out at the Canada goose family, staying together and continuing to enjoy their days with their duck friends.

After a few more weeks, another Canada goose couple came into the community. There didn't seem to be any rivalry, but the new Mr. Goose didn't want any one (goose or duck) coming close to his mate. And after a few days, Mr. and Mrs. Goose chose a spot along the wall of the south pond to lay their family eggs.

Once they had laid out various tree branches and leaves along the wall's ledge, Mr. Goose (George) decided the pond was theirs, and no one would be welcome, ducks nor geese.

The Canada goose family (now mother, father, and two babies) had made the south pond their home as well because it was the first pond they saw when they entered the community. Unfortunately, Mr. Goose (George) would not have it, and he went about it in a brutal manner.

The fighting was so unpleasant. George would fly out and jump on the back of the father goose, attempting to drown him.

The father goose would manage to get away, then George would go after the little ones.

Bird Lady ran out to the south pond's edge and intervened by swinging a broom at George. George only turned and went out after the father goose, chasing him out of the pond.

The father goose ran out of the pond and up the south pond's slope into the hallway of one of the buildings.

Bird Lady followed and found the father goose attempting to hide to stay away from George.

George remained in the pond a good twenty feet away.

Bird Lady helped the father goose out of the building, shielding him from the sight of George. She walked the father goose across the drive over to the north pond. The north pond would need to be Canada goose family's new home in order to avoid George and his ranting and raving.

Keeping the new family in the north pond was very necessary in order to keep the community calm. That same evening, the mother goose and the two little ones found their way to the father goose at the north pond. They did not want another event with George.

Bird Lady would take the evening treats to her adopted Canada goose family every day to the north pond to ensure they would not go back to the south pond. And every day, the little ones were growing and enjoyed seeing Bird Lady. The little boy goose would see her and go running with little wings outstretched in order to greet Bird Lady.

The mother and father goose looked shocked, as if to say, "Hey, wait. Don't go running around without us." But he did, and Bird Lady named him Harry. His tiny fur appeared as smooth, blond hair along his growing body. Bird Lady smiled warmly at Harry and always greeted him with a big smile and said, "Hi, my little Harry. Come and enjoy!"

There was no doubt that Harry truly loved their visits every night. Harry loved being singled out and playing with all of his friends, feathered or not!

Summer brought lots of warm weather, and unfortunately, a lot of turkey vultures started showing up because the forest around the community was almost completely gone. They no longer had a wild place to go and prey on often-unseen creatures who made the wild their home. The rabbits, squirrels, possums, snakes, and various birds were now moving into the various condo and housing communities, a short distance, to find new home. Unfortunately, some would bring hardship and destruction.

It was obvious that seeing the turkey vultures sitting on the rooftop of the clubhouse meant they were looking over the community to determine just what they might be able to feast upon.

And the turkey vultures also made it known by standing on the bank of the pond.

The following day, Bird Lady went over to the north pond to bring an early afternoon treat. Harry, the little boy goose, came running to her, as he always did, with outstretched wings, always overjoyed to see Bird Lady as much as Bird Lady was to see Harry.

In the evening, Bird Lady went over to the north pond with the evening treats, but no one was there. Bird Lady went back to the south pond, and the Canada goose family wasn't there either. Bird Lady then walked around both ponds, but no sight of the mother, father, Harry, or his sister. There was certainly plenty of duck playfulness occurring in the south pond, all waiting for their turn at the evening treat.

The next day, Bird Lady was standing on the veranda, looking out across the south pond and saw two turkey vultures throwing something up in the air. Bird Lady grabbed a broom and ran down, swinging the broom at the turkey vultures. They dropped what they were tossing about and flew off. Bird Lady looked down at what they dropped, and it was Harry. Harry made no movement. Bird Lady fell to her knees with tears flowing. The buzzards simply tortured Harry to death. Bird Lady picked up Harry and caressed his little body, running her finger across his head. Such a joyful little goose taken so early in his life, not able to fight for himself. And apparently, no one fought for him.

Heartbroken, Bird Lady buried Harry next to his sister. Kneeling over the buried little Harry, softly, Bird Lady said, "I'll greet you every night as your community of friends join you here for evening treats. Harry, you will always be remembered as the friendly and sometimes feisty little boy goose.

"And I'll also say, 'Good night, my little Harry. I'll forever miss you, my little friend.'" Unable to hold back the tears, Bird Lady walked off to find the mother and father goose.

Harry's father and mother goose were not far away. The father and mother goose, along with their last remaining child, were sitting under the trees in the south pond, looking out into the pond, as if to expect Harry to appear.

The little girl had in turn started to suffer with the short-leg syndrome that affected her sister. But she was able to waddle about and enjoy herself. They had peace and quiet. The mother was carefully watching her little girl, ready to protect her in the event of more trouble.

Later that morning, Lady Bird heard the yelling of George. George must have seen the Canada Goose family sitting across from their nesting wall. George didn't want them anywhere in the south pond. So George started ranting up again. He could be heard throughout the community, yelling.

Although George made a scene, the family didn't leave. Bird Lady walked over and saw the father and mother goose still looking out upon the pond. But where was the little girl? Looking around the grassy knoll, Bird Lady spotted the little girl. Running up to the pond's hillside to the little girl goose, Bird Lady knelt down and carefully picked up the little baby, no longer moving or breathing. In picking up the little one, it became obvious that she had broken her neck. A guess would be, George came after everyone. And in attempting to get away, the little girl goose probably tripped in having one leg shorter than the other.

Bird Lady carried the little girl over to the mother and father goose so they would know. They looked down upon the little girl, then back up at Bird Lady and turn their heads down into the pond, looking out into the pond, knowing all their lovely babies were lost forever.

As the mother and father goose remained looking out into the south pond, Bird Lady carried the last child to be buried next to her brother and sister. Such sadness was felt by Bird Lady. As she stood, looking down at each grave, she also looked over the shrub's hedge and out upon the south pond's sloping hillside.

It was the place where Bird Lady had introduced the Canada goose family to the community's south pond. The memory of the father goose running to the pond and little Harry running just behind him was still very vivid in Bird Lady's memory. They would always be a treasured memory but also a sorrowful one. If only the woodlands had been preserved as all of the buildings and apartment were constructed. But nothing was left, so all of the wild ones had to find another place to call home or find their prey, which was what was happening in what was once a very peaceful community of feathered families and friends.

Evening came, and the mother and father goose departed from the community. They would find another home away from George and rediscover happiness with family again.

Weeks later, Bird Lady noticed George and his mate were not on the ledge, sitting on the eggs. Bird Lady went over and saw the eggs were all cracked, and George, nor his mate, nor any babies could be seen.

They were quite possibly eaten by hawks or the muskrats that had started moving in.

George and his mate would continue to return for evening treats. George would also rant and rave even more than he did before, as though he now hated everyone that came into the south pond.

Although sadness had been within the feathered friend's community, they did overcome and found fun among each other once again. Some would even spread their wings even greater for new adventures ahead.

Disaster was not new to any of them, and they instinctively knew to overcome.

Throughout the summer days, the ducks were in abundance, close to a dozen mallards of every variety and sex.

There always seemed to be more boys than girls. And more often, once the girl became a mom, the dad always seemed to disappear. Not all were of that manner but enough to leave the mom to care for and safeguard the little ones.

Every evening, after the treats were enjoyed, the many varieties of ducks and Canada goose families joined each other, sitting around the south pond. It was fun to watch them looking up and down at each other, as if in conversation.

At every evening's ritual, the leader of a Canada goose family would honk out, "It's time to leave for the night," strong and loud honks, not a brief honking sound but one that was like a bugle call to attention. One evening, as one leader gave his call and started paddling out to the middle of the pond, a female duck, who had been sitting next to him, paddled alongside, as if to want to join in leading the goose family.

Her male companion stayed back for a short period but eventually paddled toward them and stopped just short of where the lead goose and duck were waiting.

After a couple more callouts, the lead goose looked back and saw his family was lining up. He looked down at the female duck and turned in a different direction, leaving her behind. He was not going to have her join. No matter what she did to attempt to join, the lead goose simply went in a different direction.

The behavior went on for days. The lead goose welcomed the female and her mate to sit next to him after evening's treat but no way when it came time to organize the family to go home for the evening.

One would think that with the lead goose turning in the opposite direction from the female duck, that would be the end of it. She would stop attempting to join. Well, think again because this little mallard female duck would not be ignored.

One evening, as the lead goose started to stand up to send out the first call, the female duck yelled out the first sounds. Hahahaha! It was not a quack quack, no.

It was hahahaha. Every time the lead goose went to make his call, she was out with the first sounds (hahahaha). For that reason, this female duck became known as Amelia—Amelia who would not be ignored. She wanted to lead the geese.

Amelia's call of hahahaha was heard for weeks. She knew to start it before the lead goose started his honk because she recognized his movements toward the pond. Who says ducks can't be smart as well as witty!

Then one evening, there were two more female ducks that joined her. Their voices were all different, so you could recognize Amelia. But then there was Millie and Katie. Amelia would start, followed by Millie, then Katie on and on, every evening.

And eventually, Amelia would paddle out. Her mate would follow along with Millie and Katie and their mates. Amelia would then lead them out for an evening fly or paddle down to the end of the pond to acknowledge time to go home for the night.

Seasons have come and gone, and Amelia continues her lead for her feathered duck friends. The Canada geese—well, they let her go first so they can then call out and be on their way.

One day, a new quack could be heard. And it was not from the Canada geese nor the female ducks. Bird Lady could always recognize the ducks' voices. It was a female mallard duck. She first didn't appear any different from any of the duck girls, or did she?

She greeted Bird Lady every day when she came to the pond's open landing, walked right up to Bird Lady to give a full view. She was a lovely female Mallard with smiling face but also an injured wing. She looked directly at Bird Lady, as if to say, "Hi, I see you today!"

Well, she was then named Mrs. Broken Wing. Mrs. Broken Wing would now join the twelve Mallard ducks that lived and enjoyed the two ponds. They all became friends. They even enjoyed the company of one Canada goose (known as Geoff), who decided he really didn't want to live anywhere else and definitely not with the geese (more about him later).

Mrs. Broken Wing's injury probably occurred while attempting to save her baby ducklings. There were no babies to be seen now. Bird Lady had seen a female duck in the north pond with five babies a week ago. And when Bird Lady went back to check on them the following day, the female duck was alone in the same spot where she kept her little ones. But on that day, she stared out into the pond, as if to think they might appear. Bird Lady didn't know where this sad duck would go next.

Mrs. Broken Wing instinctively knew to continue on after the incident. She joined the other ducks, knowing she could do all that everyone did, except fly.

The mallard male ducks could be seen picking at her wing, as if to be teasing her. But she would not have it and would chase after them. Probably, they were teasing her to get her attention and possibly her affection. It was a strange way of going about it but no bad quacks about it!

A few days later, a Muscovy duck family also arrived and joined in the fun. Actually, Mr. Muscovy arrived, and he, unlike the other ducks, seemed to know to wait for Bird Lady inside the hall at the landing. As Bird Lady came to the landing, Mr. Muscovy welcomed her by wagging his back feathers and looking directly at her. Bird Lady definitely like this fellow!

Mr. Muscovy brought along his mate. The Muscovys enjoyed the evening treat with the ducks and geese. But when Mr. Goose (George) came up to Mr. Muscovy to push him out of the area of the treats, Mr. Muscovy turned to George and, looking directly in his eyes, pulled back his head and took his beak and hit George directly on his beak.

George's head moved back and looked at Mr. Muscovy, as if to say, "Wow, dude!" Then George just walked away.

And over time, the Muscovy family size would grow and then diminish within the community to a point when they no longer lived within the community but would fly in for evening treats, then depart to safer location. They would end up losing twenty-four babies over the summer months.

But regardless of situations and experiences, they remained friends with all of the ducks and even Geoff, our loner Canada goose.

The sad situations always seemed to bring everyone together and make the best of it, all different yet enjoying the tranquility of the ponds and shade of the trees. Among them, you could always see the lanky heron, egrets, and ibis.

And there was their nonfeathered friend, Mr. Turtle, who watched the evening frolic around the treats, never bothering any-one, just watched.

As summer continued, it brought in long, warm evenings with sunlight sky until late at night.

It mattered not how late it was; the geese seemed to have an internal clock, always ticking. At just past seven in the evening, the callout to get ready to leave could be heard from each family. The V formations would start, and each family would take its turn in departing from the pond, honking out clearly a long "good night."

As autumn came into season, more Canada geese arrived. There was the family of eight, as well as the family of five. It was pretty hectic when evening treat time came. But no matter what day, every one of every feathered variety would greet Bird Lady at the landing.

Every new mother duck or goose would appear with their babies following behind. The mother duck or goose made sure Bird Lady saw the new ones who shyly followed along.

As the different Canada goose families arrived, the ducks attempted to join them in feasting on the many treats spread across the special places Bird Lady chose for scattering enough grains for everyone to enjoy. Big or small, every feathered one could enjoy. And a few times, a couple of squirrels would sneak in under the brush to pull out a few without notice.

One day, Bird Lady could be seen sitting at the side of the pond. A few of the ducks came along her side, as if to visit with her for a while. If the girl ducks made a sound, Bird Lady would recognize who she was and call out her name with a big smile and hello. Amelia was always there, along with Millie, Katie, with Mrs. Broken Wing eventually joining for a great quartet.

Time moved on, and Amelia and her leadership continued. Amelia drew together all of the ducks and Geoff, the lone Canada goose resident. Geoff didn't want to become a part of any of the Canada goose families. Geoff would only stay with the resident ducks. Geoff could be seen walking in circles along the pond or swimming in circles in the pond.

He was always watching out for a goose that may want to hurt him. Geoff must have had a very difficult time growing up within his family. So Bird Lady provided Geoff with a special spot for him to find his evening treats. Geoff was never alone enjoying the treats.

He was joined by ducks and a squirrel. They all joined together every evening.

Geoff did not walk in circles when these feathered furry friends were with him. When he did get nervous, he would start his circle walk, and Bird Lady would call him, "Geoff, it's okay. You are okay." Geoff would then walk with Bird Lady.

After many years of loving care, there came a time when things changed. One spring evening, the ducks and geese were bewildered because Bird Lady did not come down to the landing to greet them and provide everyone with the usual evening treats. The ducks and geese scurried about, looking and wondering what had happened to Bird Lady.

Amelia would sing out, followed by Millie and Katie. As the evening grew dark, everyone left.

The next couple of evenings, it was the same event. Then four days after, Bird Lady didn't arrive. Only Mom and Dad Mallard with baby duck remained, and Amelia and her two companions would fly in and sit at the pond's edge in front of Bird Lady's veranda. They knew she sat there every night, so they would wait for her. Bird Lady never came down.

The days that followed had evening light showers, as though small teardrops were falling from Mother Nature. After a few evenings, Bird Lady was extremely sad. But as the light showers continued, she could hear Amelia singing out her evening song. Then Amelia led her two companions out of the pond. But she flew them around the big tree at the edge of the community and brought them back over the pond, directly toward Bird Lady. Just a few feet from

Bird Lady's veranda, Amelia threw her wings out in flight, as did her companions, their wings fluttering to hold them straight up in flight and looking directly at Bird Lady.

Amelia held this position for just enough time to let Bird Lady know she was missed. Amelia changed direction straight down and quickly brought herself and her companions back up and out over the pond and up over the trees.

The evening showers continued with Mother Nature's small teardrops falling over the pond the community once loved and endeared by the many feathered friends that would never hear or see Amelia and the many feathered friends again.

The End of *Feathered Friends* Friendships

EPILOGUE

IRD LADY DIDN'T have a way of explaining to her feathered friends of eight years that the community's board of directors had sent her a violation notice and instructed her to stop feeding the ducks and all wildlife. The fine would be very steep if feeding did not stop. Bird Lady didn't feed her feathered friends, only brought out evening treats for all to enjoy. With great sadness, Bird Lady stopped and did not show herself in the evenings. But all feathered friends knew where she was and would look but no longer could see Bird Lady at the top.

Bird Lady never came down, so they all eventually left the community they had loved with each other and Bird Lady.

Eight weeks later, after none of Bird Lady's feathered friends returned, she decided to take a stroll along the pond. It had been difficult in the days not joining her feathered friends, many a tearful night. As she entered the last flight of stairs down to the landing, there on the landing was a young family of Canada geese with their mother and father standing proudly behind them. The mother and father goose remained and simply looked into Bird Lady's eyes to let her know they wanted her to meet their children so they might understand their love for her.

Bird Lady walked among the seven little ones, each looking up at Bird Lady and making little hissing sounds. None ran away; they all simply walked up and looked into Bird Lady's eyes and giving little hissing whispers, as if to say, "Hello, Bird Lady, Mom and Dad told us all about you. Yes, they miss you too."

After that evening, none of Bird Lady's feathered friends returned to the landing where, for eight years, they all came together to see Bird Lady come down and bring them evening treats.

A sadness and emptiness that didn't need to be, Bird Lady continues to remember and concentrate on the happy memories of her feathered friends.

FEATHERED FRIENDS
PHOTO ALBUM

Families of geese, ducks, ibis, heron, and egrets

Amelia, bottom left, with friends, Mrs. Broken
Wing with first set of babies

Family Ibis, Ibi on the lawn came every day.

Canada geese. Hey, guys, something you are not telling me?

Egret visits every evening with the mallard ducks

After evening treats, ducks and geese together
on the lawn, in the pond, having fun

Just how many ways can you turn your body?

Geoff (goose napping) with his friends

Amelia (duck at the bottom) insists on joining the geese

Amelia really likes to show off with the geese,
although they attempt to ignore her.

Mrs. Broken Wing always sat next to this fellow ibis.

Little Harry was taken all too early from this life.

Proud Father Goose watching over Harry.

Henry the heron was a regular at catching fish.

Everyone (ibis too) ignoring the "No Fishing" sign

Geoff always going in circles when afraid of those around him

Amelia sang for everyone, hahahaha.
(No quacking sounds from her!)

George, protector of his mate and horrible to everyone else

Mrs. Broken Wing after three years. She could
deal with it but could never fly.

Mr. Muscovy taught George not to mess with
him. Good peck on the beak did it!

Surprise visitor, Mr. Cormorant—an
amazing underwater swimmer

Evening sky for all to say goodbye after evening
treats and fun with each other

ACKNOWLEDGMENTS

ONCE AGAIN MY dear friend, now for over 55 years, Marla Brumley Ward, made wonderful contributions to this story. Marla, having been a teacher for many years, can find more misspelled words than Microsoft Word! Thank you Marla. Such fun sharing this story. And your suggestion to include my emotional feelings into the story caused me to grow closer to loving all feathered creatures and recognize their contributions to our lives and wellbeing. Take care of all of them. Make sure more trees, brushes and ponds surround homes, businesses and schools.

Marla and Constance
High School Seniors
Co-Captains Pom-Pom
Girls Marching Team

ABOUT THE AUTHOR

THIS IS CONSTANCE Glidden Josef's first story about the many feathered friends she came to know over an eight-year period. It isn't her first book. Her first book was a true travel adventure story. So when she shared via email with family, friends, and colleagues that a second book would be published, they all came back with similar responses.

"Oh, another true adventure story?"

"Is it about various travels throughout Egypt?"

"Hey, how about the adventure driving from Portland, Oregon, to Florida with two cats?"

"Oh, it must be about driving across the United States."

"Where does the adventure take us?"

Constance replied, "This true adventure takes place at home in Jacksonville, Florida. It's about my feathered friends."

The reply was similar among them, "So you are calling us your feathered friends?"

Constance said she rolled her eyes at the various emails and replied to all, "No, this is a true story about adventures with the geese and ducks and other birds that visited with me every day for eight years."

Everyone had known Constance and her love to travel—plus her over thirty years of experience in IT project management across the United States and various countries around the world. Everyone except one responded with a flat "Gee how fun is that!"

The one person, her friend for over fifty years, knew exactly what Constance's story could include because she had heard about many of the nightly adventures firsthand over the years. And her dear friend knew Constance would not be deterred from something she had set her mind to do. Constance always gave a good story to all of life's adventures!

www.ingramcontent.com/pod-product-compliance
Lightning Source LLC
Chambersburg PA
CBHW040112150726
48005CB00013B/1665